Instant Idea Book

Classroom Management

for Elementary Teachers

- Classroom Management Techniques
  (pages 5-37)

- Parent Communication
  (pages 38-49)

- Save Time and Work
  (pages 50-62)

  (includes reproducible pages)

by
Barbara Gruber

illustrations
Ed Salmon

NOTICE! *Reproduction of these materials for commercial resale, or for an entire school or school system is strictly prohibited.* **Pages marked "reproducible" may be reproduced by the classroom teacher for classroom use only.** *No other part of this publication may be reproduced for storage in a retrieval system, or transmitted, in any form or by any means— electronic, mechanical, recording, etc.—without the prior written permission of the publisher.*

Copyright© 1985 Frank Schaffer Publications, Inc.
All rights reserved - Printed in the U.S.A.
Published by **Frank Schaffer Publications, Inc.**
1028 Via Mirabel, Palos Verdes Estates, California 90274

ISBN #0-86734-056-8

Table of Contents

Classroom Management Techniques

Good classroom management creates a positive learning environment.

Kim
Assistant
Teacher

My Busy Boxes
Marcy L.

Busy Boxes
Name Marcy L.

Bonus Work Sheet	Free Choice	Read a Story
Math Puzzle	Puzzle Page	Draw a Picture
Write a Story	Make a bookmark	Word Cards

Busy Boxes
Name Marcy L.

Perfect Work

Awards

Trouble Shooter's Box

©Frank Schaffer Publications, Inc.

FS-8306   Instant Idea Book

Do something nice for yourself

At School

- Use recess or lunch time to take a break! Write personal notes, read a book, manicure your nails, or take a walk on the school grounds. You deserve a break!

- Avoid planning to take work home. Instead, correct papers in your classroom before or after school. Hang a DO NOT DISTURB sign on your door (so colleagues don't stop by to chat) and whiz through your work. You'll get a lot more done alone in your classroom than in the teacher's lunchroom. And, you'll find the work goes much faster than taking it home where it tends to consume your evening.

- Make certain you are not doing too much for your students. Avoid doing clerical jobs, like collating and stapling science packets. Students can do these tasks themselves.

- Find a special pal among your colleagues. It is nice to know you have a special friend. Perhaps you can pack lunch for the two of you one day this week, and your friend will bring a lunch for you the following week. Think about switching classes and teaching a lesson in one another's classes. That will be fun for you and your students.

- If someone on your staff is a constant complainer, stay clear of that person. Negative people put everyone in a "down" mood. Put on a headset and listen to rock-and-roll or Mozart.

- Do whatever you can to build a positive atmosphere. When there is a team spirit of cooperation, everyone is motivated and feels like a winner. Go for it!

- Have high expectations for your students. That makes for a positive outlook that motivates everyone!

- Give yourself a well-deserved pat on the back! On the weekend, or Monday before school, reflect upon the previous week at school. Think about things that went especially well. Identify one positive experience and write it in a notebook. Enter an item each week in your notebook. Blank books for writing from variety/stationery stores are perfect for this!

Do something nice for yourself

Away From School

- Get your days off to a great start. Fix the coffeepot, set the table for breakfast, and pack your lunch before going to bed. Gather everything you need to take to school, so you can swoop it up and be quickly on your way in the morning. Leave home in time, so you don't have to frantically rush to arrive at school on time.

- Treat yourself to a telephone answering machine. It's like a personal secretary. People can leave messages for you, and you will have fewer calls to make each evening.

- Take your address out of the phone directory. There is no charge for this. You will eventually stop getting sales calls by phone. The phone company sells a cross index to businesses which is used for telephone solicitation. Your listing will read "Your Name . . . . 555-0000."

- Block off time for yourself on your calendar every week. Make sure you do some activities you especially enjoy.

- Learn to relax. Plan a few special treats for yourself during weekend or school breaks:
  1. Go to brunch with a special person in your life.
  2. Join a group or club.
  3. Have breakfast in bed.
  4. Take your phone off the hook.
  5. Take a class (dancing, knitting, photography).
  6. Plan to exercise regularly with a friend (walk, jog).
  7. Develop friendships with people who work in other fields.

Foster independence and self-control

Solve the problem of students finishing their work at different times by providing activities for those who finish early. Allow students to choose the activities they want to do.

I'm Done!

Post a list of things for students to do when they finish their assigned work. Establish a teacher's helper center where students can do clerical tasks such as collating, stapling, tracing, cutting and pasting.

Things To Do

- bonus worksheet
- silent reading
- handwriting practice
- clean your desk
- work at teacher's helper center
- extra credit book report
- encyclopedia quiz
- write to your pen pal

Busy Boxes

Give each student a manila envelope containing a grid with nine empty squares and a grid with nine activities. Students choose an activity to do in their spare time. When they have completed three horizontally, they turn them in to be checked. A star is placed on the blank grid for each activity that was completed. When the blank grid is filled, the student receives an award. *(Ideas for awards appear on pages 22-26.)*

You can select new activities for each month or season.

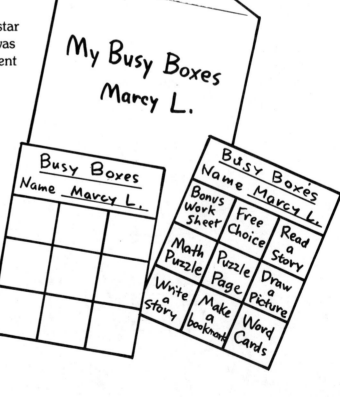

Foster independence and self-control

Fixing the Fidgets!

It is difficult for many children to sit still during story time or while watching a film. Try these techniques to fix the fidgets.

• Play Clay

Allow each student to hold a ball of clay while listening to a story. Students can pinch, poke, and squeeze the clay as they listen. At the end of the story time, collect clay balls in a dish pan.

• Fuzzy Friends

Each child may bring a stuffed animal to school. These fuzzy friends are kept on a shelf and may not be touched without your permission. During story time, students may hold their fuzzy friends. Provide a few extra stuffed animals for students who cannot bring one from home.

• Reading With a Friend

Tell students to get out their silent reading books when they finish their work. As long as they continue to read, they may have their fuzzy friends on their desks.

Foster independence and self-control

Say It Again!

When you are giving your class directions, say the direction and ask the entire class to repeat it aloud.

Silly Questions!

Many students waste time with dependent behavior. When students ask unnecessary questions, redirect the question back to the student.

For example:

(student) I don't understand this.
(teacher) Show me the part you don't understand.

(student) I don't get this.
(teacher) Show me exactly where you are stuck.

(student) Is this right?
(teacher) How do you feel about it?

(student) Where is my pencil?
(teacher) Where do you think it might be?

(student) I'm done, what should I do now?
(teacher) What do you think you should be doing?

(student) Can I sharpen my pencil?
(teacher) What is our rule about sharpening pencils?

(student) When is it time for lunch?
(teacher) When do you think it is time for lunch?

©Frank Schaffer Publications, Inc.

FS-8306   Instant Idea Book

Foster independence and self-control

Establishing Class Rules

Brainstorm with your class about rules that should exist in your classroom. Jot all ideas suggested by students on the chalkboard. (When you are brainstorming, jot down **all** ideas. There are no wrong answers.) Then, discuss the ideas and narrow the list down to as few important rules as possible. Post this list of rules. Duplicate class rules for students to show to parents.

Make the Most of Every Minute!

Before dismissing the class for recess or lunch, have students get out materials needed immediately after the break. Then, when students come in, you can begin your lesson promptly.

Keep It Snappy!

Maintain a lively pace in your classroom. Have established procedures for getting help, lining up, giving out materials, sharpening pencils, etc. Start lessons promptly and run the classroom in an orderly fashion. When students have to wait, it provides an opportunity for misbehavior to occur.

Improve concentration with exercise

Get Energized With Exercises!

Perk up your class with chair exercises done to snappy music. An exercise break is a change of pace that promotes concentration. You may want to illustrate each exercise on a chart. Then, line up exercise charts along the chalk ledge in the order you will do the exercises. Choose a student to lead the group. Do the exercises with your class. It's fun and good for everyone!

Try these exercises. (Repeat each exercise four times.)

1) Clap   Snap   Touch shoulders   Knock on desk

2) Touch shoulders   One arm to the sky   Touch shoulders   Other arm to the sky

3) Lift one shoulder   Lift the other shoulder   Lift both shoulders

4) Right leg   Left leg   Both legs

Improve concentration with exercise

5)   Arms out,   Roll fists   Stretch fingers   Make fists

       make fists   over   out   again

6)   Clap   Shake (3 times)

7) Elbow-to-knee—
    Interlace fingers behind head.
    Touch left elbow to left knee,
    lifting knee and bending at waist.
    Then touch right elbow to right knee.

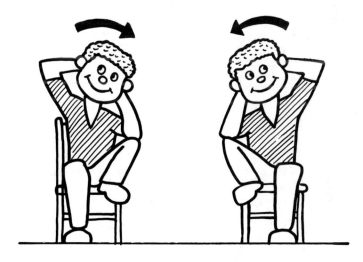

8) Place your hands against your head above the ears.
    Bend head to the right,
    exerting slight resistance with hand. Return.
    Repeat movement to the left.

©Frank Schaffer Publications, Inc.

FS-8306   Instant Idea Book

Managing student behavior

When a student misbehaves, you can:

- Look at the student.
- Send a silent signal. *(See page 18.)*
- Walk near the student.
- Touch the student's desk or shoulder.
- Call on the student to respond.
- Speak briefly to the student.
- Move the student to a different desk. *(See "Quiet Work Zone" idea below.)*
- Have the student telephone his/her parent.
- Telephone the parent.
- Send home a sign-and-return note. *(See page 21.)*
- Hold a parent-student-teacher conference.
- Hold a parent-student-teacher-administrator conference.
- Begin using a behavior card to report to the parents. *(See page 21.)*

Quiet Work Zone

Ask the custodian for a few extra desks. Establish a work zone where no talking is permitted. Add cardboard study carrels to each desk to screen out visual distractions.

Managing student behavior

Make Every Student Respond

Instead of calling on one student, use the every-pupil-response technique. It encourages every student to pay attention.

- When asking students true/false questions, ask all students to put thumbs up for true, thumbs down for false.

- When going over a list of words on a worksheet, ask students to read aloud like choral speaking.

- When going over a list of words on a worksheet, ask students to underline, circle, put an x in front of, or draw a box around certain words. For example: Circle the word with three syllables or underline the word that rhymes with jumps.

- Ask all students to write down their answers to your question, then call on one student to read his answer aloud.

- When you are going to call on a particular student, don't say the name of the student before your question. If you say the student's name, only that student will pay attention to the question. Ask the question and all students will begin thinking of an answer, then call on one student to respond.

Reading Tag!

Keep your readers on their toes in the reading circle. Divide your group into two teams. Whenever you call on a student to read, her team earns a point if she knows the place. The team with the most points at the end of the week earns a reward. *(See ideas for rewards on pages 24 and 25.)*

Let's Chat!

Just imagine how thrilled your students would be to have a three-minute chat with you that is free of interruptions. At the beginning of each week, mention to two or three students that they will have a turn to chat with you during that week. (That gives students a chance to think about what they may want to discuss.) Hold a three-minute chat giving students a chance to talk to you while you sit back and listen, then respond. Keep track on a class list, so everyone has a turn.

Jot a List!

This is an interesting exercise to do when you are away from school. On scratch paper, jot a list of the names of your students from memory. Some students will pop into your mind immediately. And, there will be some students you have trouble remembering. Those students whose names you jotted down first get most of your attention. And, those on the bottom of the list are probably getting less attention than they deserve. Now that you know who those students are, try your best to make sure they get their fair share of your time.

Managing student behavior

Broken Rules

When a student breaks a class or school rule, have the student write down what happened. When three violations have been recorded, her parent must sign the record of the violations.

Breaking Bad Habits

Help a student break a bad habit by using tickets to monitor the number of times it occurs. For instance, to a student who constantly gets out of his seat, give four tickets that permit him to leave his seat during work time for the entire day. Each time the student leaves his seat during work time, he must give you one of his tickets. Gradually reduce the number of times the student may get up by giving him fewer tickets.

Act It Out!

Hold a class discussion about difficult situations such as rudeness or cheating. Elicit from students a variety of appropriate ways to handle such situations. List possible solutions on the chalkboard. Then, have students role play appropriate solutions to the problem.

Managing student behavior

Silent Signals

Invent some silent signals to use with students so you can communicate non-verbally.

For instance:

- touch your watch
  (when a student is wasting time)

- touch your ear
  (when a student is not listening)

- touch your mouth
  (when a student is talking too much)

- hold up your pencil
  (when a student should be writing)

- hold up a book
  (when a student should be reading)

Telling and Reporting

Explain to your class the difference between telling (a nice word for tattling) and reporting (explaining an important situation that could hurt someone). When a student comes up to tell you something, ask if they are "telling" or "reporting." If they are telling, ask them to write you a note about the incident. (Most students will not want to bother.)

Are you telling or reporting?

©Frank Schaffer Publications, Inc.

FS-8306   Instant Idea Book

Managing student behavior

Let's Think It Over

Announce to your class a particular problem you want to discuss later that day. Ask students to start thinking about possible solutions without discussing their ideas with others. You might want to write the problem on the chalkboard. Then, when you are ready to discuss the problem, students will be prepared.

Trouble Shooters

Have a "trouble shooter's box" (an empty tissue box works well) located in your classroom. Students can jot a note about a problem they feel the class needs to solve and put it in the box. Notes in the "trouble shooter's box" may be written anonymously. Select problems from the box for discussion. Write each problem on the board, discuss it and elicit ideas from the class to solve the problem.

Ask the Experts

Select four or five students to be on a panel of experts. Have the panel sit in the front of the class, facing the audience. State a class or school problem, or read one from the trouble shooter's box. Ask each expert to propose a solution to the problem. Then have the class vote on which solution is most workable. Keep track of panel participants on a class list so everyone has a turn.

Managing student behavior

Disagreements Between Students

Before attempting to solve a disagreement between students, have each student fill out a disagreement form. Filling out the form allows a cooling off period for students and provides an opportunity for the parties involved to come up with solutions.(*See the reproducible form on page 21.*)

Behavior Contracts

A behavior contract is used to monitor the behavior of a particular student. It is more effective when parents are involved. Hold a meeting with the student and include parent(s) if possible. Identify the problem and discuss specific behavioral changes that are necessary. Write out an agreement and have all parties concerned sign it. Keep the behavior contract on your desk top where you won't forget to record behavior. Send the contract home daily for a parent to sign and return. If parents are not involved, perhaps you can have the student take the behavior contract to the school office to be signed at the end of each school day. (*See reproducible behavior contracts on page 21 and weekly notes for parents on page 43.*)

Disagreement Form

My name is _____ Date _____

I have a disagreement with _____

We disagree about _____

_____

What happened? _____

_____

Two ways to solve the problem are : (1) _____

_____

(2) _____

The problem is _____

_____

To solve the problem, I agree

to _____

_____

_____

Date _____

(student) _____

(teacher) _____

(parent) _____

Sign-and-Return Note

Behavior Contract for ☺

_____

Week of _____

(day)	(teacher's comments)	(parent sign & return)
Mon.		
Tues.		
Wed.		
Thurs.		
Fri.		
Notes:		

a reproducible page

Rewards to motivate students

Award Certificates

Make or duplicate award certificates at the beginning of the school year. Clip together all the certificates that are alike and place them in an envelope with a class list. Whenever you give a student a certificate, check the student's name on the class list. This will help to keep you aware of which students have received recognition.

Sprinkle Rewards Along the Way

When your students are working through a multi-step assignment, sprinkle a few awards along the way. For example, if students must complete sixteen phonics packets at their own pace, duplicate a reward chart for each student. Students use the chart to record their progress. It is motivating to work toward short-term goals and to record specific progress.*(See ideas for rewards on pages 24 through 26.)*

Rewards to motivate students

How Much Did You Earn?

Cut out pink construction paper piggy banks, paper wallets, or bank books for your students. Use coin stamps to stamp "money" the students earn for good work. Money can be spent on rewards or for items in a class store. *(See page 24.)*

Happy Smile Cards

On Monday, give each student a happy smile card for the week. Students may earn a maximum reward of three tickets daily. Use a paper punch to punch cards under the happy or unhappy faces during the school day. Students earn a ticket for each punch under the happy face. However, each punch under the unhappy face means one less ticket. At the end of the week, students spend their tickets on rewards or at a class store.

My Happy Smile Card		
Day	☺	☹
Mon.	★	
Tues.	★	
Wed.		
Thurs.		
Fri.		

Rewards to motivate students

Class Store

Have students bring items to donate to the class store such as toys, puzzles, and books they are permitted to give away. Save items until you have enough to open a class store. Ask other teachers if they have any items they want to donate. Add items such as a few pencils, pieces of construction paper, or boxes of crayons to the store's merchandise. You, or a committee of helpers, can determine the number of points/money/tickets needed to purchase each item. "Prices" should be placed on each item.

Open the school store at the end of the week or at the end of the month. Having the classroom store open for business can be used as a reward for the entire class.

Rewards for the entire class

- Work extra business hours for the classroom store.
- Enjoy an extra P.E. period.
- Show a film. (Let students vote which film they want you to order.)
- Receive an extra recess.
- Do a special art project. (Let students vote.)
- Have 10 minutes of free time.
- Listen to radio during work period. (Vote for the station.)
- Go to lunch five minutes early (escorted by teacher).
- Extend lunch period by ten minutes (supervised by teacher).
- Watch a television show.
- Have an extra period in the school computer lab.
- Have an extra period in the school library.
- Have a popcorn party.
- Choose a field trip.
- Hike around school grounds.
- Enjoy a brown bag picnic.

©Frank Schaffer Publications, Inc.

FS-8306   Instant Idea Book

Rewards to motivate students

Rewards for individual students

- Have fuzzy friend on student's desk during work time. *(See page 9.)*
- "Work" in the classroom store.
- Have a "cut pass". (A pass that allows students to cut in line one time.)
- Be Assistant Teacher. *(See page 28.)*
- Choose an award to present to another student. *(See reproducible award tickets on page 26.)*
- Lunch with your teacher.
- Keep score during a game.
- Call out words during a spelling bee.
- Change a bulletin board.
- Take attendance for the day.
- Bring something (hobby) to show to the class.
- Be excused from one workbook page.
- Sit in a different seat.
- Lunch with a friend.
- Extra library visit.
- Check out classroom game to take home.
- Choose three pieces of art paper to take home.

©Frank Schaffer Publications, Inc.

FS-8306   Instant Idea Book

_____
(Student Name)

has earned a ticket for
a 3-minute talk with teacher.

_____   _____
Date   Teacher's Signature

_____
(Student Name)

has earned a ticket to
sit in a different seat for 1 day.

_____   _____
Date   Teacher's Signature

_____
(Student Name)

has earned a ticket to
help the teacher teach a lesson.

_____   _____
Date   Teacher's Signature

_____
(Student Name)

has earned a ticket to be
excused from one homework
assignment.

_____   _____
Date   Teacher's Signature

_____
(Student Name)

has earned a ticket to
be first in line.

_____   _____
Date   Teacher's Signature

_____
(Student Name)

has earned a ticket to
be first in line.

_____   _____
Date   Teacher's Signature

_____
(Student Name)

has earned a ticket to
cut in line 1 time.

_____   _____
Date   Teacher's Signature

_____
(Student Name)

has earned a ticket to
cut in line 1 time.

_____   _____
Date   Teacher's Signature

a reproducible page

26

©Frank Schaffer Publications, Inc.

Active involvement for students

Increase student participation by sharing authority with your students. Involving students in making decisions is an excellent way to build trust, and let students know you want them to have an active role in the learning process.

Your Opinion, Please!

Describe two activities or projects to the class. Allow students to vote to determine which one the class will do.

Have a crazy-mixed-up day when students vote on the order in which subjects will be taught on that day.

Why Are We Learning This?

It helps all students to know why they need to learn a particular skill. Whenever possible, share with students the purpose of a task or lesson. For instance, in order to be successful with division problems, it's important to know the multiplication tables.

Whoops . . . I Made a Mistake!

Explain to your class that errors are a part of learning. Tell students that you expect them to make errors in the process of learning. Use yourself as an example by sharing with students errors you have made in learning something new. Students find it reassuring that everyone makes mistakes when he or she is mastering something new.

©Frank Schaffer Publications, Inc. FS-8306   Instant Idea Book

Active involvement for students

Assistant Teacher

Select a student to be "Assistant Teacher" each day. That student dismisses the class for lunch and recesses.

Row one is dismissed!

My School Box

Ask students to establish a special place at home where they put things they must bring to school. Once students get in the habit of taking items from their "school boxes" as they leave each morning, there will be fewer forgotten items.

Suggest that parents NOT bring forgotten items to school for their children. Remembering homework, lunch money and library books is the child's responsibility.

The Buddy System

Encourage your students to help one another. Assign each student to a partner in the class. When a student is absent, the partner is responsible for gathering all the work that is passed out for the absentee.

©Frank Schaffer Publications, Inc. FS-8306   Instant Idea Book

Active involvement for students

Long-term Goals

Elementary school assignments are usually due at the end of the work period or the school day. Train your students to be responsible for long-term assignments, too. For example, at the beginning of the school year give students an assignment that is due on December 1. In January, make an assignment that is due at the end of the year. This helps students learn to deal with long-term assignments. *(See "The Encyclopedia Quiz" on page 61.)*

How To Succeed in School

Discuss study skills with your class. Elicit ideas from students about techniques that work for them. List information on the chalkboard. From the list, make up a How-to-Study List. Post the list on a chart and duplicate it for students to take home.

How to Study
1. Find out what is the best time of day for you to study.
2. Study in a quiet, neat place.
3. Don't study when you are tired or hungry.
4. Don't study while watching television.

Active involvement for students

Share the secrets of success with your students. You may want to list success tips on a chart or bulletin board and duplicate a copy for each student to take home.

Things to do before school:

1. Get enough sleep at night.
2. Eat breakfast before school.
3. Bring necessary things to school.
4. Arrive at school on time.

I'm glad you had a good breakfast!

Things to do at school:

1. Use your best handwriting.
2. Read directions carefully.
3. Be a good listener.
4. On tests, do easy questions first. Skip problems/questions you can't do.
5. After finding as many answers as you can, go back and attempt difficult problems.
6. Use extra time to check your work.

Long, Lost Paperwork!

Keep track of missing assignments the easy way! When required work is not turned in, have the student fill in a "Something Is Missing" form. Send these forms home for parents to sign and return. Keep these forms handy to include in parent-teacher conferences.

Something Is Missing!
Name _____
Date _____
Missing work: _____
_____
It is ☐ lost ☐ late ☐ other.
Reason: _____
_____
Please sign and return.
_____
Parent's signature   Date

©Frank Schaffer Publications, Inc.

FS-8306   Instant Idea Book

Active involvement for students

Self-evaluation is an excellent means for sharing responsibility with students.

How Do We Rate?

When students work in groups, appoint a leader for each group. At the end of the work period, the group leader fills in the group evaluation form about the group's work. *(See the group evaluation form on page 32.)*

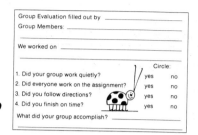

I Did My Share!

To make sure each student in a group is participating, have each group member fill out an individual evaluation for group work. *(See "I Did My Share" form on page 32.)*

Goal Setting

Setting goals enhances one's sense of personal power. Ask students to identify one specific area where they want to improve. Have students use a goal-setting form to identify the steps they will take to reach their goals. This technique comes in handy for teachers, too! *(See "My Goal" form on page 33.)*

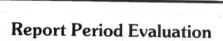

Report Period Evaluation

A week or so before report cards are issued, give all students the "My Progress Report" form. Ask students to use the first column of numbers to indicate areas where they want to improve. Collect forms and have a brief conference with each student. During that conference, indicate the areas where you feel the student should improve in the other column. *(See the progress report form on page 33.)*

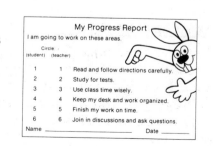

Group Evaluation filled out by _____

Group Members: _____

_____

We worked on _____

_____

Circle:

1. Did your group work quietly?   yes   no

2. Did everyone work on the assignment?   yes   no

3. Did you follow directions?   yes   no

4. Did you finish on time?   yes   no

What did your group accomplish? _____

_____

🐛 I Did My Share! 🐛

_____   _____
(Name)   (Date)

Our group worked on _____

_____

Circle:

I worked quietly.   yes   no

I followed directions.   yes   no

I finished on time.   yes   no

I worked on _____

_____

_____

About My Work

	yes	no	sometimes
Do I work quietly?	___	___	___
Do I follow directions?	___	___	___
Am I a good listener?	___	___	___
Do I take turns?	___	___	___
Do I share materials?	___	___	___
Is my work neat?	___	___	___

I need to work on _____

_____

_____

_____

_____   _____
(Name)   (Date)

©Frank Schaffer Publications, Inc.
FS-8306   Instant Ideas Book

My Goal

My goal is _____

_____

_____

To reach my goal, I will:

1. _____

2. _____

3. _____

Signed _____

Date _____

My Work

Name _____

Date _____

Assignment _____

_____

_____

Circle:

I finished on time.	yes	no
My work is neat.	yes	no
My work is accurate.	yes	no
I followed directions.	yes	no

My Progress Report

I am going to work on these areas.

Circle:

(student)	(teacher)	
1	1	Read and follow directions carefully.
2	2	Study for tests.
3	3	Use class time wisely.
4	4	Keep my desk and work organized.
5	5	Finish my work on time.
6	6	Join in discussions and ask questions.

Name _____ Date _____

©Frank Schaffer Publications, Inc.

FS-8306 Instant Idea Book

Building team spirit

When the entire class is working toward a reward, there is a team spirit of working together. Keep it positive by recognizing good behavior and good work, instead of subtracting points. (Ideas for group rewards appear on page 24. A list of things for which to give points appears on page 36.)

The One Hundred Grid

Make a grid on tagboard or the chalkboard with one hundred squares. Color in squares to recognize good behavior by individual students or groups of students. When the grid is completely colored in, the class has earned a reward.

100 Grid

Our reward is a movie and popcorn.

A Jarful of Popcorn

Pop a batch of unbuttered popcorn. Put the popcorn in a paper bag and keep it in your closet. When the class has earned a "point", drop a kernel of popped corn into a quart-sized mayonnaise jar. When the jar is filled, the class has earned a popcorn party. Then pop a big batch of corn for the party.

©Frank Schaffer Publications, Inc. FS-8306 Instant Idea Book

Building team spirit

What Is the Score?

Designate a spot on the chalkboard where you keep track of points earned by the class. When the total reaches one hundred, the class has earned a reward. Each day, jot points on the board to form a column addition problem. At the end of each day, record total points for the day.

The Scoreboard

Mon.   27
Tues.   19
Wed.   24
Thurs.
Fri.
Total

Today
6
2
4

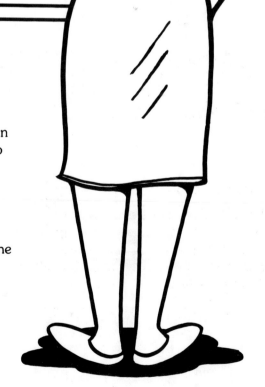

The Mystery Envelope

Put each student's name on a slip of paper in a "mystery names box." Each day draw five names. Place those names in an envelope and place it in your desk drawer. Do not look to see which names were drawn.

When a student breaks a class or school rule, write that student's name on the chalkboard.

At the end of the day, read the names aloud from the envelope. For each name read aloud that is **not** written on the board, the class earns a point or another kernel of popped corn in the jar. (See popcorn idea on page 34.)

Building team spirit

Behaviors for which the class can earn points:

- point for each student who turns in homework, five extra points if all students turn in homework
- coming in the room quietly after a break
- leaving room quietly for lunch or recess
- point for each clean desk, five extra points if all desks are clean
- point for each student who turns in a long-term assignment (like a book report) by due date, extra points if all are in by due date
- good behavior on field trip
- good behavior during library lesson
- good behavior for substitute teacher
- working quietly
- neat papers
- point for each signed permission slip returned on time, five extra points if all come back on time
- good behavior in cafeteria
- good behavior during fire drill
- good behavior during assembly
- good behavior during film
- room cleaned up quickly and quietly after art lesson
  (See ideas for rewards on pages 24 through 26.)

My, what good behavior!

 **My ideas for classroom management . . .**

Parent Communication

Parents want to know what is happening at school. Here are some sure-fire, easy-to-implement ideas for parent communication. Parents will give you an A+.

Communicating with parents

Communication Cards

At the beginning of the school year, make a communication card for each student. Jot each student's name and phone number on a 5" x 8" card. Arrange the cards in alphabetical order and fasten with a rubber band. Keep the cards in a handy spot. Whenever you make an extra contact with a parent by phone or note, jot it on the card. The cards are an easy-to-keep record of communication throughout the school year.

Scott Peters
555-1234
10/5 note about eye test
10/22 mrs P. called about test-he is getting glasses

Ready-to-Go Envelopes

Jot each student's name on an envelope and place envelopes in your desk. Put them in an obvious spot where they won't be forgotten. Once or twice a week, pull out an envelope and jot a quick positive note to the parents of that student. When you have used all the envelopes, each student will have taken home a positive note in a ready-to-go envelope.

Stationery stores are a wonderful source of free envelopes. After a holiday, unsold cards are returned for a rebate, but the envelopes are usually discarded. Ask the store manager to save them for you.

Communicating with parents

Names and Notes

Fold a piece of 12″ x 18″ construction paper like a wedge and place it on your desk. Write one student's name on the name tag. Be especially observant of that student for a day or two. Jot positive observations on the name tag. After you have written several comments, give the student the name tag to keep on her desk for the day. Then the student can take it home. Keep track of names on a class list, so everyone has a turn.

Homework Assignment Book

Provide each child with a notebook. When you assign homework, students write the assignment in their notebooks. Students show completed homework to a parent who signs the notebook. When you check homework at school, you can write comments in the notebook, stamp it, or make a check mark to show that the work was turned in.

Take-Home Learning Materials

Allow students to check out learning materials such as textbooks, games, charts and maps to show parents what they are studying at school. Keep track of borrowed materials on a class list. Students who enjoy playing school especially enjoy borrowing "real" materials from school.

©Frank Schaffer Publications, Inc. FS-8306 Instant Idea Book

Communicating with parents

In Search of Excellence

Have each student decorate a "Best Work Folder." Keep folders in a box, so they don't get crumpled. Every week, each student selects one sample of what he considers to be his best work and places it in this folder.

"Best Work Folders" can be given to parents at your school's open house or with report cards. If time permits, allow each student to select one sample from his folder to show to the class.

Weekly Work Packets

Do you send home a folder of completed work with each student on Fridays? In many busy households, that folder is ignored or gets "lost in the shuffle" of weekend activities. Try sending work home from the previous week on Mondays instead of Fridays. You will find that parents pay more heed to the child's work when she will be returning to school the following day. Give it a try!

Instant Parent Communication

Before starting a new unit of study, inform parents about the unit by letting them review the assignment. For example, if you are starting a unit on ecology and you have a contract and packet of activities for students to do, tell the class about the ecology unit. Then have students take the unit folder home for parents to peruse and sign. Then proceed through the unit of study in the usual manner. Parents love being "in the know," and students enjoy telling parents about the upcoming unit.

Name _____ Started: _____	
Ecology Unit Done: _____	
Things to do	Date Done
Science Book pp.31-39	
Questions p. 40	
Vocabulary Test	
Water Experiment	
Food Chain Chart	
Filmstrip	
Poster	
Extra Credit: _____	
Evaluation:	
Please sign and return.	
Parent _____ Date _____	

Communicating with parents

Weekly Progress Notes

Communicate the quick way with weekly progress forms. Use instant progress reports with all your students. They are especially helpful in maintaining good behavior prior to holidays or vacations when students tend to let behavior slip. *(See reproducible progress notes on page 43.)*

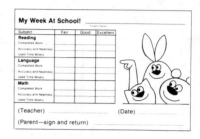

- Use progress notes every week in December or at the end of the school year. They will help your students maintain a high level of productivity.

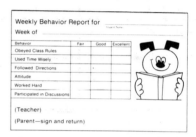

- Send notes home one week with boys and the following week with the girls. Then you have only half as many notes to fill out each week.

- Pick one week each month to send home progress notes. Don't tell students which week it is!

(If you need to monitor a particular student's behavior, see page 21 for behavior contract ideas for individual students.)

Personalized Stationery

Design your very own stationery to use for note writing. *(Or use the reproducible notes on page 44.)* Buy a ream of mimeo paper in a cheery color for duplicating note paper. Parents will quickly spot your notes when students bring them home.

My Week At School! _____
(Student Name)

Subject	Fair	Good	Excellent
Reading			
Completed Work			
Accuracy and Neatness			
Used Time Wisely			
Language			
Completed Work			
Accuracy and Neatness			
Used Time Wisely			
Math			
Completed Work			
Accuracy and Neatness			
Used Time Wisely			

(Teacher) _____ (Date) _____

(Parent—sign and return) _____

Weekly Behavior Report for _____
(Student Name)

Week of _____

Behavior	Fair	Good	Excellent
Obeyed Class Rules			
Used Time Wisely			
Followed Directions			
Attitude			
Worked Hard			
Participated in Discussions			

(Teacher) _____

(Parent—sign and return) _____

©Frank Schaffer Publications, Inc. FS-8306 Instant Idea Book

To: _____

From: _____

Date: _____

_____

_____

_____

_____

_____

_____

_____

_____

A note from _____ **Date:** _____

To: _____

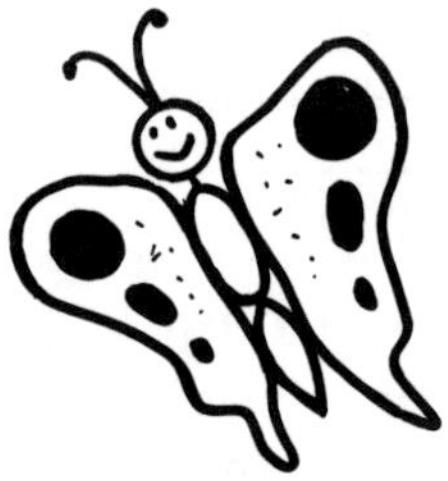

_____

_____

_____

_____

_____

_____

_____

_____

©Frank Schaffer Publications, Inc.

FS-8306   Instant Idea Book

Communicating with parents

Thumbs Up!

Share this handy technique with parents and students! To determine if a book is at a child's independent reading level, tell the student to hold up his hand as he reads one page. Each time he encounters a word he cannot read, he puts one finger down. If, by the end of the page, his thumb and four fingers are down, the book is too difficult. If his thumb (or thumb and some fingers) is still up, the book is not too difficult. "Thumbs up" means the book is okay for the student to read independently.

Home Learning Activities

Give your students an opportunity to earn points for out-of-school learning activities. This program can be used all year long or for just one month. It is a wonderful activity for months when children are kept indoors by nasty weather.

To use the reproducible "Home Learning Activities Calendar" on page 46, add the name of the month, dates and the list of activities that students may do to earn points. Each student who wishes to participate takes home a copy of the calendar. The parent records activities done by the child throughout the month. At the end of the month, calendars are returned to school. Students receive an award for the points they earned.

(See ideas for rewards on page 25.)

Mommy, look at this!

Home Learning Activities

Home Learning Activities

_____ (month)

_____ (name)

Sunday	Monday	Tuesday	Wednesday	Thursday	Friday	Saturday

Parent—Sign and Return: _____ Date: _____

©Frank Schaffer Publications, Inc.

FS-8306   Instant Idea Book

Communicating with parents

School Handbooks

Duplicate a school handbook for each student to take home. Parents will appreciate having this handy reference about school. Perhaps your school administrator or parent group will take on this project. It could be sent home with the eldest child in each family to avoid families receiving multiple copies.

Be sure to include:

Daily Schedule

—tell earliest time students may arrive

—recess times

—lunch

—dismissal times

School Staff
(names of)

—principal

—nurse

—school secretary

—librarian

—your name and school phone number
  (Tell parents how you can be reached. Suggest leaving a message with school secretary.)

Procedure for Reporting Absences

Procedure for excusing students from school appointments

Map of School
(Show where your classroom is located.)

School Calendar

—holidays and vacation periods

—conference or report dates

—open house dates

—last day of school

(If parents have this information early, they can plan appointments and vacations, so their child does not miss school.)

Communicating with parents

How Parents Can Help Children Learn

Parents will appreciate receiving a list of activities that will help children learn. Parents will find this list to be especially valuable before a vacation period and as a list of things to do instead of watching television.

- Help your child get a library card for the public library. Find out from the children's librarian if there are special children's programs for your child.

- Look through your child's schoolwork with him. Let your child tell you about his work. Perhaps your child can make a scrapbook at home with samples of his best work.

- Listen to your child read.

- Read to your child. Children of all ages enjoy hearing stories.

- Establish a reading time for your child such as after dinner or before bedtime.

- Read the comics' section of the newspaper with your child.

- Help your child select television shows to watch.

- Watch a television show together, then discuss/evaluate the show.

- Watch and discuss television advertising with your child.

- Teach your child how to make an emergency phone call.

- Help your child learn his address and phone number.

- Show your child how to use the telephone directory.

- Show your child the location of your home on a map.

- Play a board game with your child.

- Help your child start a collection of rocks, stamps, pressed leaves . . .

- Give your child his very own calendar.

- Write notes to your child.

- Help your child write notes and letters to relatives/friends.

- Subscribe to a children's magazine for your child.

- Help your child cook something.

©Frank Schaffer Publications, Inc.

FS-8306   Instant Idea Book

My ideas for parent communication . . .

©Frank Schaffer Publications, Inc.

FS-8306   Instant Idea Book

Save Time and Work

Here is the help you need to get organized and stay that way!

Time-saving tactics

Try these secrets of success for effective communication!

- **Learn to say "no" and mean it!**

  In most groups and clubs, there are a few people who do most of the work. If you have taken more than your fair share of turns at heading the social committee or being the PTA representative, say "no" to extra-curricular tasks until everyone on the faculty has had a turn. Simply say "no" without feeling guilty or giving a long list of reasons why you are refusing. When you give reasons and excuses, it dilutes the strength of what you are saying.

- **Learn how to get what you want!**

  Use the "broken record" technique to get what you want. Keep repeating your position without backing down or making excuses.

  For example:

  (principal) "Miss Sunshine, you will be the social chairperson for one more year, right?"

  (Miss Sunshine) "No, I'm through with that task. Please pick someone else."

  (principal) "Oh . . . you always do such a great job. Surely, we can count on you for just one more year."

  (Miss Sunshine) "Thank you, I did a good job. However, I will not accept the job for this year."

  (principal) "Well . . . you sound pretty sure that you don't want the job."

  (Miss Sunshine) "Yes, that is correct. You need to select another person to be social chairperson."

- **Ease the pressure by putting people on "hold."**

  Distinguish between urgency and emergency situations. When you are pressed to say "no" or do something and are not ready to do so, say:

  "I'll have to get back to you on this first thing tomorrow."

  "I need time to think it over. I'll get back to you."

  "I'm feeling pressured when you give me a time limit. I need a chance to think about this. Let's talk tomorrow after school."

©Frank Schaffer Publications, Inc.

FS-8306   Instant Idea Book

Time-saving tactics

Learn how to work smarter, not harder!

- Set reasonable daily goals. Don't pressure yourself to do more than is humanly possible.

- Don't let your job consume your life. Establish certain hours as work hours and pursue other activities with the rest of your time. *(See ideas on pages 6 and 7.)*

- Organize your desk and work area so you don't spend precious time searching for things. *(See page 56.)*

- Don't allow yourself to get over-committed, so you have no time left for yourself. *(See page 51 for how to say "no.")*

- Make the telephone work for you. Call a parent ten minutes before the bell rings, so you have a time limit for the call. Learn how to get off the phone when calls take longer than they should:

  "The bell is about to ring, thanks for your time."

  "I need the next three minutes to review our science lesson."

  "The principal needs to use the phone."

  "I'm out of time. I'm glad we had a chance to talk."

- Get a realistic perspective on worries and emotional issues.

  Ask yourself what the importance of a particular concern will be a month, six months or a year from now?

  Ask yourself what is the worst possible thing that could happen?

  Learn to compartmentalize your life. Start thinking about being the best teacher possible the moment you set foot on the school grounds. When you leave the school, close that compartment in your head and go on to other things. If you are worried about a meeting next Tuesday, do not allow yourself to start thinking about it until that day. That way future or past worries won't kill your effectiveness every day.

- You are Number One! *(Don't miss the list of ideas on pages 6 and 7 for how to do something nice for yourself.)*

Time-saving tactics

Paper Folding

Asking students to fold their papers a certain way can be confusing and time consuming. Try the hot dog and hamburger methods described below.

Hot Dog

When you want students to fold their papers into four columns, tell them to fold it like a hot dog.

Fold it in half.
Fold it in half again the long way. (Hot dogs are long.)
Crease folds.

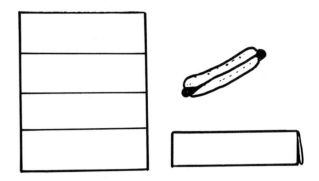

Hamburger

When you want papers folded into four sections, tell students to do hamburger paper folding.

Fold paper in half.
Fold it in half again so it comes out square. (Some hamburgers are square-shaped.)
Crease folds.

Half-a-Hamburger

Half-a-hamburger results in a paper folded into eighths.

Fold like a hamburger.
Now, fold it in half (like half a hamburger).
Crease folds.

©Frank Schaffer Publications, Inc.

FS-8306   Instant Idea Book

Time-saving tactics

Save Time Correcting Papers

- Record below-passing grades in your gradebook in a different color, so they stand out.

- On math papers, circle wrong answers.
  After student corrects the problem, write a "K" next to it. Now it is OK.

- On math papers, highlight wrong answers with a yellow highlighter. When students make corrections they can easily locate problems that need to be corrected because they are highlighted. When papers are returned to you for rechecking, you just look at highlighted problems.

- After a writing assignment (like writing a paragraph about a famous person), divide your class into four groups. Each group is in charge of editing papers for different kinds of mistakes. Papers are passed from group to group. When a student gets his own paper back, it has been proofread for errors in punctuation, spelling, capitalization, and has been read aloud. Proofreaders indicate (in pencil) on the paper where they think errors exist. They write a "P" for punctuation error, "S" for spelling, "C" for capitalization, and a "?" if when the paper was read aloud, something didn't sound right (missing words, repeated word). Give students a few minutes to look over their proofread papers and make any corrections with which they agree.

- If your students do a particular task each week that takes you a great deal of time to correct, have the girls do it one week and the boys the following week. That way, you only have half as much work each week.

- Give each child a red pencil to use for corrections. After a math assignment, have students put away their regular pencils and get out their red correcting pencils. Students circle in red any wrong answers as you call them out. After checking papers, students may get out their regular pencils and rework problems that were wrong. When you collect papers, use a blue pencil to mark problems (circled in red) that are still wrong.

Time-saving tactics

Do some lessons every day that result in no papers to correct!

- After reading a story in the basal reader, ask comprehension questions for students to answer orally. Make lessons complex by asking students:

    "Do you agree with that answer?"

    "Who can give me another answer to that question?"

    "Can you prove that?"

    "Why is that a good answer?"

- After reading the story in the basal reader, have students write three questions about the story. Hold a discussion during which students get to ask their questions and call on someone to answer.

- Make up sets of flashcards for words for math problems. Let students work with a partner and test one another.

- Do silent math with your class. It works for addition, subtraction, multiplication and division. It is a perfect activity when you are waiting in line, or just have a moment or two before the bell rings.

Teacher holds up fingers:

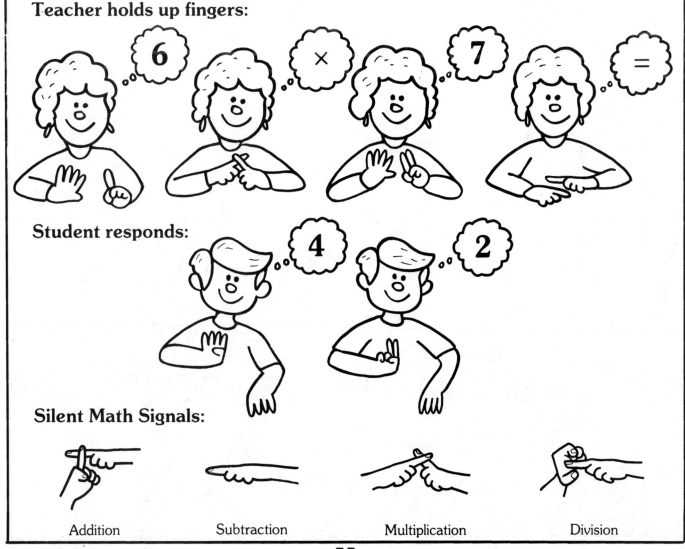

Student responds:

Silent Math Signals:

| Addition | Subtraction | Multiplication | Division |

Let's get organized

Super Sorter

End searching for lost papers forever with a "Super Sorter." All you need is a shoe box and some file folders. When you have a telephone call to make, slip it in the phone call folder.

phone calls

notes to write

read later

take to office

next week

next month

must do today

take home

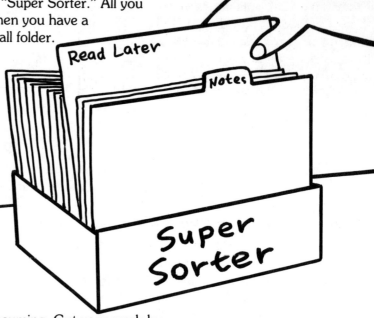

Homework Hassles

Creating homework assignments is time consuming. Cut your work by standardizing homework assignments. For example, tell the students what their homework is for every Monday and Wednesday for the entire school year. Then you only have to create assignments for Tuesdays and Thursdays.

Monday: Cut out a news article from the newspaper. Paste it on a paper. Write a sentence telling who, what happened and when.

Wednesday: Write a sentence for each of your spelling words.

©Frank Schaffer Publications, Inc.

FS-8306   Instant Idea Book

Let's get organized

The Nine O'clock News

Write announcements you need to make to the class on the chalkboard. Tell students they are responsible for reading the announcements when they enter. Or, appoint a student announcer to read the announcements aloud.

It's time for the 9 o'clock news...

Handy Dandy Substitute Folder

Label a file folder "For Substitute" and place it in the front of your desk drawer. When you have worksheets you didn't have time for that week, pop them into your sub folder. Keep an eye out for things to stash in that folder. Then, when you need to plan for a substitute, you will have some ready-to-use activities.

The Big Jobs!

Is it time to clean out your file cabinet and discard that unit on Howdy Doody from the fifties? Instead of taking a sabbatical leave to accomplish the task, scale it down into segments. Put a construction paper marker in your file cabinet and every week go through a small section and move the marker back. Eventually you will have worked your way through and accomplished a big job that seemed insurmountable.

Do the same thing at home when it comes to house cleaning. Do one closet a month (a year?). In real life, there is no such thing as "spring" house cleaning.

Let's get organized

Our Bulletin Board

Designate one bulletin board in your room as a student-decorated board for the entire year. Divide students into groups and make out a schedule for the year, so each student has an opportunity to be on the bulletin board committee. Post the names of the students who have worked on the bulletin board beside their display.

One to One Hundred Page Check List

This is an easy contract that works for any subject. Duplicate a "generic" contract that is numbered from one to one hundred. To keep track of completed pages in a workbook, duplicate a copy for each child and staple inside the front cover of the workbook. When page 33 is completed, mark it off on the check list inside the workbook cover.

All-year-long activities

Save time and work by establishing some activities that can go on all year in your classroom. Here are six activities to get you started.

The Talker's Club

Divide your class into four groups. On Mondays, announce what the Talker's Club Topic will be for that week at school. After lunch on Tuesday, students in that group get to talk to the class for two minutes on the topic. Use a timer for this activity.

Have a suggestion box, so students can suggest Talker's Club topics.

Letter-of-the-Month

Have your students write letters to a different person or organization each month. Put all the letters in one manila envelope for mailing. Display whatever you get in return for the letters on a bulletin board.

For K-1 students, use a piece of chart paper to write a group letter. Discuss the letter and have students dictate sentences for you to write.

Some interesting places to write:

Office of the President
The White House
Washington, D.C. 20001

Authors of children's books—
write to author in care of the publisher

Chamber of Commerce
for cities, states, or countries
(Ask for addresses from your local chamber of commerce office.)

TV Shows—
write in care of the network:

CBS Television City
7800 Beverly Blvd.
Los Angeles, CA 90036

ABC Television Center
4151 Prospect Ave.
Los Angeles, CA 90027

NBC TV
3000 W. Alameda Ave.
Burbank, CA 91505

©Frank Schaffer Publications, Inc.

FS-8306   Instant Idea Book

All-year-long activities

The Poetry Club

Post a poem on a bulletin board on the first day of each school month. Read the poem to the class and encourage students to memorize the poem. On another day, you might have the class read the poem aloud together. When students think they might have memorized the poem, they can say it from memory and receive a sticker if they can recite it perfectly.

Change the poem on the "poetry club" bulletin board each month. You will be delighted at how proficient your students become in memorization.

Before taking the poem down on the last day of the month, have students make a picture about the poem.

Have your students copy the poem of the month as a handwriting activity. Poems can be compiled into a poetry book.

As soon as a student can recite the poem, allow that child to listen to others recite the poem. You might want to list a few "poetry club listeners" on the board, so children know to whom they may recite the poem.

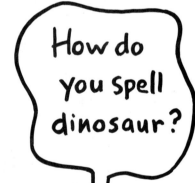

Theme-of-the-Month

Select a subject that your students will find interesting. Make that topic the theme for the month. Have an interest table where you display materials and books about the topic. Encourage students to bring items to share that relate to the theme. Create a bulletin board, show a film and read to the class about the topic. If possible, write a letter to get information. *(See page 59.)*

Have a suggestion box for the students' ideas of themes for upcoming months. If you get a lot of suggestions, have students vote to select themes for the future.

All-year-long activities

Extra Credit Book Reports

Set up a book report center, so students may earn credit by doing extra book reports. At the center, have book report forms and a list of various book reporting activities.

Encyclopedia Quiz

Dust off that set of old encyclopedias for this activity. If you don't have a set, check with the librarian to see if the school has any old sets of books no longer in use. Look through each volume and jot three questions on a card that can be answered in that volume. Paste or clip the card inside the cover of that volume. Tell students that this is an activity they must complete before the end of the year. This is a perfect activity when students are done with their work. A student takes an encyclopedia volume to her desk and finds the answers to the questions on the card in that book. Show students how you want them to present their answers to you, so they are easy to correct. Keep track, on a class list, of which ones students have finished. *(See Long-term Goals on page 29.)*

My ideas for saving time and work . . .

©Frank Schaffer Publications, Inc.

FS-8306   Instant Idea Book

Notes . . .

©Frank Schaffer Publications, Inc.

FS-8306   Instant Idea Book